Gallery Books
Editor Peter Fallon
HERE COMES THE NIGHT

Alan Gillis

HERE COMES THE NIGHT

Gallery Books

Here Comes the Night
is first published
simultaneously in paperback
and in a clothbound edition
on 16 September 2010.

The Gallery Press
Loughcrew
Oldcastle
County Meath
Ireland

www.gallerypress.com

ISBN 978 1 85235 494 7 *paperback*
     978 1 85235 495 4 *clothbound*

A CIP catalogue record for this book
is available from the British Library.

Contents

for Rosie

Down Through Dark and Emptying Streets

Open a new window.
Go on and Google yourself.
Open Facebook and update
all trace of yourself.

While you search MySpace,
sync your apps, correct a wiki,
blah blah on your blog,
tweet and stream, you see

such-and-such has got in touch,
requesting you as a Facebook friend.
And the name's slow-dawned gravity
widens the window, weirds and sends

you plunging into the déjà vu
of a phlegm-skied twilight
with unreal soldiers on the walls
lit by fire-red and air-blue streetlights;

sends you trampling through the fank
and crumble and Regal packets
of your hedgeless estate
in a tarnished and tufty leather jacket,

flappered and frazzled paisley shirt,
scuffed and shagged-out oxblood boots,
walking away from your mother, the screech
of your sister's wee black flute,

past the clanking monkey bars,
swings and roundabout of a dog-dark
dungeon of a playground,
through a sinister elm-guarded car park,

cutting to the main street through
the grounds of a windowless factory,
past the pockmarked and *Jesus Lives*
walls of the public library

while the sky turns to liquorice,
dull cardigan and tobacco fumes
embered with persimmon blushes,
melon-flowers, mango blooms;

walking until you catch a hint
of her toe-to-heel click-clack
and follow her past scuppled shops,
dead-end alleys, hokey flats;

past head-the-ball hardnuts driving by
in souped-up Cortinas and Capris
hunting their prey; and she's driving you
doolally, knocked at the knees

as you follow her past the bookies'
arcade machines and nudgers'
Fisher-Price lights and beep-bop-bings;
past the queue of scratching pudgers

in the chip shop where a pouty girl
shovels cod with a lizard-eye
love bite, Princess Diana pendant
and powdered-over black eye;

past chain-smoking bars with ducktape
on the cracks of their panes
silhouetted by the awful size
and dormant metal of dockyard cranes;

and you're all hearts and flowers
with each step into the square,
where she turns so you can finger
her pampas-bleached and hair-

sprayed hair, and she says Hey there,
in her clown voice, is that a spanner
in yer works? under the twenty-foot
high frown of an *Ulster Says No* banner

and her ribcage is delicate white
as flour on a fillet of fish
while her lips, still hot with sausage,
salt and malt vinegar, mouth a wish

and clarty newspapers carry news
of the weekend's nil-nils
windblown with Special Brew
cans and Styrofoam cups as you thrill

to her octopus fingers,
the probe and prod of her plum of a tongue,
your teeth and her teeth tapping together,
holding breath until kingdom come.

She asks will all this last forever?
against the dun Woolworth's door.
Now your hard drive hums and haws.
You waver between *Confirm* and *Ignore*.

In the Shadow of The Mournes

The wind gowled at windows, howled through hedgerows,
     uprooted a dead-rooted tree;
the full moon looked like a full moon does
     in a Hammer Horror DVD;
the road was a scar on the curving neck
     of high heathered fell and drumlin;
        and Johnny Black came driving,
     gear-grinding, jack-knifing,
Johnny Black was soon arriving
     at The Devil's Coach Road Inn.

He wore a Hugo Boss leather jacket
     and tight cream Diesel jeans,
his Dolce & Gabbana t-shirt was a v-
     necked peppermint green.
He wore Converse shoes, ribbed Calvin Klein whips,
     dangled a Camel between his lips,
        and he drove a Beemer,
     a jet-black gleamer,
a five-gear screamer with maximum bling that'd he fling
     from nought to ninety in a blip.

It was 3:30 am, the bar was shut, he parked
     fifty yards down the road.
The wind whammed into a corrugated shed
     so you'd think it about to explode,
yet he sallied like an alley cat to the back-
     yard door, and who was waiting there,
        but the owner's daughter
     Kylie with raven-black mascara
smudged by rainwater running down the eaves,
     down through her raven-black hair.

Now Kylie was married and only helped
        her Da pour the Guinness
when her husband, Danny White,
        went away on business.
But his business wasn't kosher, it was Columbian.
        He had the run of every local town.
                You didn't screw
        with Danny, everybody knew
you'd be worse off than black and blue:
        the most murderous misdemeanant in South Down.

Danny had his doubts and had Mad Dog Frank
        spy on Kylie, to fish for anything fishy,
staked out on a hill with his pit bull Francis
        in a beat-up brown Mitsubishi
to report on any ballyhoo. So Mad Dog Frank was slobbering
        over his usual stakeout dreams,
                when the pit bull
        Francis pulled and drooled
at you-know-who, wrenching Frank from the willow-switch
        and snatch of his Hungarian whiplash Queen.

'Hang in tight, sugar doodle. Don't worry, I'm on
        for a windfall tonight.
I'll be back at five, and then we'll take off on
        the first Magaluf-bound flight.'
Johnny kissed her wet mouth, her lush curving neck,
        thinking he was clever.
                Back in his car he zipped
        off lickety-split
like a bullwhip and ripped straight for Danny's hush-hush
        coke deal outside Rostrevor.

Mad Dog Frank pushed Francis the pit bull away.
  He was starting to feel the stress.
He thought of Kylie's hips and curving haunches in her soft
  long sapphire split-leg dress,
her flaming lips, ravines of raven-black hair
  and the snow-white avalanche
    of her breasts.
  Yes, in his best
dreams he'd nest smug and snuggle there forever.
  Mad Dog Frank was Special Branch.

He'd worked undercover for five years, starting in Belfast,
  then Newry city
on small-time deals using Francis the pit bull
  for don't-fuck-around authenticity.
Now in a top crew, knowing what Danny could do
  with any old kitchen knife,
    he was on the brink,
  about to sink
him but all he could think of was the avalanching sapphires
  of his flame-lipped and rainwater-hipped wife.

Mad Dog Frank guessed green-eyed Danny had lost the plot
  with his paranoid suspicions of Kylie
and ignored him, hoping for a flash of her flesh-coloured tights
  when she reached up for the expensive brandy.
Now he rubbed the big O of each eye, thinking it over.
  Johnny Black? Who would ever
    have guessed? But he thought it best
  to act fast and get the arrest
now lest Danny shot or strangled or stubbed her:
  so he called in the deal near Rostrevor.

Danny White was cold and hard,
        Johnny Black all heat and bluster.
Black was barely twenty-one, White was old school,
        ex-quartermaster.
White was careful, Black was hasty,
        the two together would surely be tasty.
                White had courted Kylie
        for five years while he built a tidy
ceasefire operation. She'd straddled Black within an hour
        in the back of a blue A4 Audi.

At 4:14 a Special Unit moved in on Danny
        and his dealers.
At 4:18 Johnny was too cooked to take mark
        of all the peelers'
unmarked cars, and burst in thinking this was *Heat*
        and he was Al Pacino.
                He fired a shot
        from his sawn-off shot-
gun and promptly took one in the head, while Danny was
   riddled,
        acting like Robert De Niro.

Seven years on, Frank works in Liverpool and sleeps,
        if he sleeps, in his car,
off his face on dirty money, pimping immigrants,
        throwing big tips at bright tits in a Hooters bar.
Monthly he pays for humiliation and the willow-switch
        of a heroin-eyed Hungarian whore,
                haunted by shrivelled wreaths,
        shovelled knees and knuckled teeth
grovelling under broken noses, grot and snatters
        on a raven-black Carrickfergus shore.

He thinks of red diesel runs under spilt milk skies,
        debt collections in ice-bound caravans,
Mickey Finns and schoolgirls, ringed pit bull fights,
        migrant worker scams,
camouflaging stashes in ramshackle barns
        with sheep bleating abattoired and ardent.
                He thinks of Kylie in Magaluf
        with her Polish chef
under the thatched roof of her Irish tapas bar
        and adjacent beachfront apartment.

Sunsets, Zombies, Screwdrivers, Sours,
        Harvey Wallbangers, PG tips tea:
she still provokes a polka, serving vodka and cola
        while men still leer with shit-faced subtlety.
She thinks of her hard working Da
        and her long dead Ma who lies
                in the shadow of The Mournes
        under bent firs and whitethorn
as the soft air teases a crinkled smile below her wrinkled
        snow-white nose in the sunrise.

But at night she thinks of 5:00 am, when the wind bawled
        in addiction and grief;
when dirty Frank emptied himself of the ambush,
        Danny's money, his own raw heat on his knees;
when the road was a scar on the curving neck
        of high heathered fell and drumlin,
                and Mad Dog came driving,
        blind-riding, soon colliding
through the raven-black rain, under an unreal moon,
        into The Devil's Coach Road Inn.

In Whose Blent Air All Our Compulsions Meet

1

Put your clothes on, she said, you're not dead
yet and we must take the air, and so on.
Yah de yah de yah. And so, we take the air.
When summer nettles with sunblaze and pollen,
when birdsong crackles like a salesman's cold call,
when fizz-fuzzed may bugs bizz-buzz — blah blah blah,
when we've gone to seed, sickened by our sequel
(falling fruit in the laughing livid air):
it's time to *do-re-mi* through the day's *fa-so-la-ti*,
its music of movement, scored by shadows.
No car, nor bike, nor bus, but one
foot following the other to a field or wood-
land as the town disappears, to conclude
where sycamore leaves shiver in the sun.

2

How the mind drifts, as we mosey along
through brief nights and long walks in public
parks or by shorelines, by the riverside's
crinkled ferns and fronds, traipsing past
hawksbeard and hawthorn, the brambled
hedge-banks of the cindertrack; how the mind,
as the melony sunblaze spangs bangles
over windlebrooke and witch-hazel that waggles
and sways while the breeze blows wild garlic
and you pull your hair back to the music
of the moment; how the mind plays away
and other times and places take shape and surface,
fuse and fester in your mind's shifting frame
you chase through again, and again, and again.

3

It's a funny thing how the same old things
can take the eyes from your head; how empty
rooms alter through days that flash by like bliss,
or string themselves out like a la-di-da
lecture on thrift in a dull banker's office.
It's funny how fine dust gathers; how the sound
of each wave's crash and suck-back into the hoo-ha
of the sea can soothe and creep under your skin.
And your eyes are black, your eyes are brown,
as dark as the night that ravens to frame
the fairy lights of a far-out Christmas town.
It's funny how I'll enter a room, fresh as mint,
cock a snook with the sun, and the look
in your eyes says, well, it's yourself, again.

4

I remember lamps, logos, suits and pants
in shopfronts as you pulled me to an entrance
and had me high as a cloud over High
Street until you burst me like a balloon.
I burst, and at first I fell slightly like spittle
off a tongue, a muckless moongrey mizzle.
Then I sploshed, splooshed and sizzled
until hurled harum-scarum from the sky
like Crazy Golf golfballs, Looney Toons
eyeballs bouncing up and down the street.
And your skin was sleek as a tight Speedo
swimsuit as we holed up in the atrium of a Tesco.
I always want to purl down your cheeks,
quiver in the gutterstream between your feet.

5

We walk, and our legs tick-tock toward fire
or that rift in the ground where dusted lilacs
and wild teasel are growing among windblown
cellophane, used Featherlites, discount flyers;
and still we put our best foot forward
to trek our winding cindertrack under blue-red
sweeps over dead heathered hills, by a high-walled
trinity of partly-scrubbed street slogans that show:
'Vote for Sin', 'Fuck the Pop', 'God is go'.
Later in the dusk we'll crash and tune in
to the drone of our head's hive and honeycomb
of sun-gilt and dark evaporation.
Sometimes it doesn't help knowing
there is more than one way of going.

6

Now we toe the line towards nostalgia
for long unfurrowed nights and easy days
in green sloped gardens, Black Magic and dahlias,
the exactitude of taste in the measure,
tone and timing of spontaneous compliments,
the gradual revelation of fetishes
and nuanced interpretations of implicit messages
hinting at monogyny until death.
I might say these are the mere husks of habits
implanted by use like these words, or any words,
turning us to puppets. But then you'd point up
to the wrens, smallest of birds, sweeping the breadth
and buffets of the sky, flittered and fluttered
on a whim, on a buck-and-wing of breath.

7

Going for a pop song, going to pot
in a Homebase bed of jasmine and bergamot:
when you reach over, and your shadow spews
over my bent of mind, I want to do with you
what darkness does with candlelight,
what an egg whisk does with an egg white,
what the blazes of sunlight do with the sycamore,
what a well-oiled hinge does with a back door,
what a whetstone does with a Kobayashi knife,
what the postman's second ring does for a flagitious wife,
what Castrol GTX Magnatec oil does with a V8 engine,
what the wind does with wrens high on a buffet and whim
    as they spiral and swoop and hover and spin;
then you reach over, your eyes pursed and finite,
and blow out the candle. Here comes the night.

8

In the morning we wake and board the bus
packed like a waiting room for a passport
or injection, then pass into our grave
and buckled grid of concrete and bustled
compartmentalization and feel the eyes
of silent police within the workplace,
the long arms of check-outs that cordon
each store, bars clamping alarmed doors
against dirty sneakers with Burger King beakers.
In some such way we dreep through the day
as the hours wind down. We talk for minutes,
then go under to our dreams' self-harm
to haggle with the quick and the dead,
the wards of night, waiting for the alarm.

9

Dreaming of murder, dreaming of kites,
dreaming of leather that fits good and tight,
of thighs and hot tongues from morning to night;
dreaming of widgets, of television,
dreaming of first place in a competition;
dreaming of Havana, of counter-intelligence,
enormous mojitos, a forbidden entrance;
dreaming of fire and sword upon parched veldt,
rain-swept gorse, shattered windows, shattered delft;
dreaming of a trophy wife and hyperbolical wealth,
a peachy brand new brand name blushing on the shelf;
dreaming of hawks, dreaming of doves:
between the weird filth below, blasted wonder above,
dreaming a sentence in the cells of love.

10

My love is a mansion with many rooms to see.
I'm asbestos.
My love's a glittering surface, scrubbed spotlessly.
I'm the germ that can withstand Domestos.
My love's a Penelope rose. I'm the canker.
My love is Independence. I'm the Union.
My love is a passenger and I'm the wanker
sat next to her, eating egg and onion
sandwiches, saying 'I'm no right-winger, but . . . '
My love is a peach. I'm its hard nut.
My love's an open threshold. I'm the dark within the door.
My love is untouched land. I'm a shovel. Go dig.
My love's a high-minded principle. I'm its war.
Come to think of it, my love is a prig.

11

We turn to each other, time after time,
the way shoppers in a strip-lit superstore
reach for the daze of familiar brands;
the way wrens return to their element
having scavenged the earth to its shore;
the way we bear ourselves through thin air
that lifts the scent of scutch grass as my mind
drifts up my rear end to spew from my mouth
once again, into the mayhem of herky-
jerky mayflies, as we hobble, hirple and head
down the cindertrack past maybells and bellfowers
to the shade of the sycamore's branches
while hysterical wrens scuttle and ganch
in tongues of purple fire overhead.

12

We take the air, it has no surface, it has no depth;
but the air won't cease to put another crease
upon your changing face, in the corner
of your eye. As our slow path turns to dewed grass
and the pixel-rich sky thrums we reach our tree
while an aeroplane cuts the mustard of the sun
in the song-stained air. With mayflies jigging:
this is your life. May bugs buzzing: no real
harm done. Ferns and leaves dancing. And your dress
is burnt sienna, you breathe the shade's perfume;
a wren breaks free, your face lights up — a may-apple
in bloom, or an open book. With shadows twitching:
look, everything's moving. Raw earth turning:
you're not dead yet. The livid air laughing.

Looking Forward to Leave

There were sliced-beef brown-bread triangles,
boys on one side, girls on the other side,
hair claws, white socks, rashed necks strangled
by tight top buttons and crooked ties,
beakers of dull orange that dirty Chris gargled
before nudging: *which one ye goanna ride?*
And when I tried to learn to dance for you
my fingers marked your forearms red and blue.

Then there were bluecoats on one side, redcoats
on the other side, a battle of the bands,
banners waving in the sun, black flutes, eight-carat-
gold signet rings, a line drawn in the sand,
balmorals, plumes and epaulettes, taunts and gloats
over hard-drilled drums. And when I raised my hand
to fight for you, my eye flamed hot flamingo
pink, then gloamed to a stoned avocado.

But on Basra's streets there are no clear sides,
just dust and heat-hazed aftershocks, infrared
sensor systems, suspect cars we've pulled aside —
you'd think their eyes would pop from their heads
once they've eyed me, although I'm mostly inside
the Warrior, or in barracks with hotheads
blasting hardcore beats that would drill your head:
hole in your head, in your mutherfucking head.

We move north to what they all call *the shit*
tomorrow and I'm unsure when I'll next return
to your emails without the entire unit
looking over either side of me at the screen,
but I'll be keeping a diary, to write it
all down, each dream in which I burn
to song-flames, poppies and embers,
leaves we might walk through this November

when the leaves, flared to fire-colour, take leave,
fall into memory; for there is a book
of books we all carry inside, its leaves
crisply turning, and I remember that look
in your eyes when, before I left, you laughed —
there's magic in the music and the music
is in us — I read in that look for some such
meaning, in this desert, my make-up smutched.

Another unmarried woman with a child
has been taken, beheaded, purified;
and I live for my leave, when I'll slide what you called
my un-be-fucking-lieve-able legs either side
of you. I look forward to nothing but the cold,
cans of Harp and soda farls, my hair newly dyed,
the soft skirt I'll wear, the music we'll play,
and we'll get hammered on Remembrance Day.

Graduation Day

The bluff, heave and hill-slide of Arthur's Seat
turns butter-drippled green and streaked fox pelt,
then glouts back to crow blue and gristle grey.

It weighs on the edge of the mind
and rings with the hills of Edinburgh
to frame the eye, as crowds dressed to the nines

in jet brogues and stiletto heels
note the tricks of light on architecture,
spires and domes of black Binnie shale

and Craigleith sandstone, raised on free trade
and the slave trade. At Dreghorn Barracks,
also, new recruits are filed on parade

as the sky turns from cobalt to blu-ray
and forty-faced hills turn three new shades
of green-brown-grey, as if to say

you've arrived at the beginning of a chapter
not yet written: to all these in display
gowns and uniforms, smiling to be captured

in digital frames, bursting to enter
the fray, where they might flit swifter
than the hills which, yet again, gizzen and gley

as if to say there's a time to get and a time to lose,
a time to keep and a time to cast away:
to those in closing-down offices and dole queues

who watch these graduates stream into bars
like cowslips, tormentils and may-
bloomed hawthorn along a springtime loan,

as if such words might stay the ring of hills
from pressing like hands around a throat.
But the sky lifts again and the hills

unearth new green from forty shades of grey,
girthing us together, to be second-guessed
no more than those put-upon, who smile upon

fresh faces bringing new reason to say
forgive us our debt. Today we have
begun to plant and we await the harvest.

Fledglings

An unseen force lifts the lid off
our sleep and powers the planted roots'
push to brief wonder. How much of
heaven and atoms do we grasp
before, as a matter of course,
we are cast on four winds and give
up the ghost? Like lemmings lined up
under a razing sun we cross
over to the dark side of the force.

The Debt Collector

Between the anticipation and aftermath,
the trickle of water and quenching of thirst,
between the wish and what comes out in the wash,
the seed packet and gladioli bloom,
between now, then and when,
all you know will vanish down the plughole.

No matter how ripe the fruit in the bowl,
erotic the violets, erratic the stars,
at night empty rooms gather you in their claws.
Their silence licks you. All that is lost,
all that is botched streams into one strange image
in the mirror and wears your eyes.

Darker by the day, you feel a stranger
hover at the window, eavesdrop on your calls,
at your shoulder in darkened corridors,
head bowed two seats ahead of you on the bus,
in the shade of the lindens and silver limes,
adept and ready, wearing white gloves.

On a bare wall the clock face ticks.
That you were never liable is a myth
like easy money. So live accordingly.
The hours are long, the months disappear,
and the moment nears when he will come.
He will speak with your voice.

Only if you're lucky will he come without hurt,
steal into your borrowed home
and lead you through this town's coil
of limbs and longing, bear you through the rain,
along nameless roads to a green wood
whose river weaves its murmur with conifer song.

There he'll lay you down in the riverweed,
clubmoss, hazel scrub, witch butter,
covered in a shallow night of crawling soil.
So make the most of your loan, though all that
is gone, or is going, will never let you go.
In our deaths our debt will grow.

Prelude

Soon enough you start to wonder
who you are, ache to reach within,
clear the clutter and discover
your exact life, the real thing, the looming
contours of yourself from core to brim.

You enter a room rid of everything
but paper, pen, couch, slim volumes,
Bushmills, coffee, a stack of CDs
and a succulent. You wait to begin.
Soon enough you start to wonder.

You thought in space and silence the hub
of yourself or the moment or the thing
in itself might orbit, but the thing is
there is no silence, but a bluebottle's huzz
and a creak on the stairs, though no one's there.

You doodle. Doze off. Come to.
Murder the Bush. Sloom off again.
Wake up in darkness and wonder
where you are. The water pipes are rats,
the wind against the window is water.

The door is open. There's a mirror
in the landing but you don't realize
and blench at its glim of noctilucous
light in the gloam. You are drawn
goose-fleshed towards its lurid glare

when something hideous lurches from there.
Your eyes clamp tight. Though not turned on,
the stereo suddenly squawks into song.
Voices start to rise, murmur and creep
from the walls. You peek an eye to peer,

but now the walls have disappeared,
and the voices grow louder to babble
and trattle over karaoke country
ballads, for you've found yourself stranded
at a party where people wear Sarah Palin

plastic masks, their skin like clingfilm,
and they turn on you, laughing and gawping,
glaring at you. They are turning to eyes.
They are nothing but eyes, a swarm of wasps
boiling towards you, each one a jewel

or a star, many stars, a galaxy
of seething, ravenous fulguration
on a canvas of venom as your head
peals in dark matter and you yawl and mewl,
but the sole sound now is of wind or water.

Then she appears, like the moon, out of nowhere,
and the thing you were after suddenly
becomes the thing she once whispered to the swoon
of your ear, her mouth's tincture, the melting
of her eyes, her calligraphy in motion

as she turns away. You follow her through
the hall, a garden, down a twisted lane
to creep through hushed rain and high grass,
but you've lost her. Everywhere there's a hiss,
a voidance, a crackle rising like mist

from the green and the graves, and you succumb
to these revenants and succubi of sound,
running in rings that circle no thing,
no nothing: you are ghosted from bone to skin,
nerves, pulse, waves rising, falling within.

Soon enough you start to wonder
who you are, ache to reach within,
clear the clutter and discover
your exact life, the real thing, the looming
contours of yourself. You enter a room.

In a Nondescript Town

Gulls crawk and cry over rooftops and sirens,
evacuated schools, outraged streets, fire engines,
while families hunch and huddle in their drives
watching TV crews, news reporters gather.

Tight-lipped plainclothed officers sip coffee
on a floral sofa. A neighbour explains:
'When he stared at you. As if he'd cat's eyes.'
His mother slumps alone in the kitchen.

A tap drips. Light glades her still head.
Upstairs on the landing a detective
breathes deep, pushes the 'Do Not Enter'
sign of the bedroom door and takes it in

as if standing on the threshold of hell,
trying to make sense of a small made bed,
flat screen, consoles, notepads, posters,
so many books stacked neatly on their shelves.

Rush Hour

Going here, going there, getting nowhere
in late October, as elm leaves divorce,
rustle and swish, scattered through the air,
wind-driven down a four-lane via dolorosa —
I've lost the plot, chasing the ghost of a
pattern to falling parts, a swirl of fictions,
one clinging tight to each leaf in the air.

The only haven I have found,
waiting for what goes around to come around,
is this caged bridge across the carriageway,
with tall city lights on one side and low
estates on the other, where I've come to bay
above the two-way come and go
of car lights half-cupped in the twilight.

Blustered by open gusts and gulped air
above the traffic, I puzzle the gap
between myself and the *nnyaao, nnyaao, nnyaao*
of these cars on credit, sidewindered by the spree
of zooms and fumes, windscreens and chrome gleam,
high-styled capsules of inner calm
at death-force speed, holding their course,

hissing and heaving to a steamed glut
and gulder of lava through the canyon —
a flavid liquid mainlined into one vein
scalding through the smogged air —
as the ever-coming cars rush on,
their wonders inside, their violence passing
into the tyre-streaked and sundropped horizon.

I count the cars and coaches going under
this caged bridge across the carriageway —
a Scalextric track of trucks and trailers,
SUVs, HGVs and MPVs — imagining
if they drive far enough west they'll end
up coming back at me from the east
like the tide coming in, looping home

movies, memories made actual,
flesh and blood in metal steering home.
But if they drive far enough west they'll end
up in Ayr, or Stranraer, filled with doldrums
and sandwich-stink, gut-busters
turned butt-gusters, cranky at black waves
crashing shoreward, spuming hoodlums.

To one side of me, tall business towers
cut their veins, ooze warm people:
the city's aerial masts, steeples and spires
stand forlorn as giant props on an empty set
where the playwright's lost the plot,
stocked his car with whiskey and set out west,
looking for a link between head and heart.

To my other side, bored gangs dribble beer
cans and stone the slumped schools of their estates,
gathering to taunt, scattering to hide
from a scrunted widow who wheezes and teeters
with wild-ringed eyes through the thicket
of hedges, sealed houses, their wonders inside,
clutching for dear life her lottery ticket.

The on-going tail of this on-coming traffic
looks like a monstrous trail of army ants,
memory-void machines on the march,
numberless and numb, venomed and spuming —
each car, with its contents, an untold story:
unknown, countless and speedy-bye-bye gone
in a long snaking unstopped drone and throng.

I often picture myself in a Jaguar
with all the mod-cons, kids singing in the back,
their mum sharing wine gums with the radio on;
but as we drive on, and on, I can't ease
off the pedal, juggernauting faster, faster,
until the wife and kids shrink to horror-struck
strangers with cooked-egg eyes: *Please. Mister. Please.*

Over the elms, and towers, and terraces sail
fast shadows, last streaks of the sundrop's fall
on the caged bridge's sprayed slogan —
We Kill to Live and Die Forever —
falling on what has been done and can never
be undone, on the out of work returning
empty-handed, on the stone-eyed, on a snogging

couple who drift into the lilac elsewhere
of the sky, where crows circle in a constant
present tense, gliding into the past,
preying over tawny leaves, windblown on the tar,
squidged against the windows of a happy-hour
party in a low-eaved roadside bar
where they will pass, into the night, like these cars.

As the hurt moon raises its hinky eye
the haunted bank towers give the heebie-jeebies
to the city: their glimmerous portents sweep
across the suburbs like banshees or zombies
with anchovy skin and pistachio eyes
in a child's recurring dream, or debt
threats looming in the guilt-blushed sky,

while I skulk on this bridge, on my road home,
before I'll put on my bright mask and alight
on the thrawn clump of my estate, to creep
past alleyways, crescents of drawn blinds,
hooded glints, returning to my dark
hall, closed bedroom doors, my frightened
child's murmurs in the pale terraced night.

But now I watch the traffic pass like money,
rats in a sewer pipe, blood in my veins,
hiddy-giddy with constant burling sound
on this caged bridge across the carriageway,
waiting for what goes around to come around
as blown leaves swirl, bustle and itch
to be born again, taken by the toxic ground,

the inflamed sky, contaminations the night
will not cure, while the wind stops and starts
across this shaken bridge and the rush
hour burns between the tall city lights
of the head and low estates of the heart,
burrowing into late October's elsewhere,
going here, going there, out of nowhere.

In These Aisles

From an ASBO to Asda
I've come a long way, they say,
as if stacking shelves was a
big dream of mine, like 'wey-hey,
it's Spreads and fucken Preserves today',
although it would, in fact, be okay

so far as such shit goes, I suppose,
if it wasn't for the likes of her
with her coriander and nose
in the air, her sun-tinted spikes of hair,
crashing into me like some charioteer,
like the fact I'm simply standing here

working my gonads off is some grave
insult, like it's big of her to brave
these rough aisles — some muckamuck
with a River Cottage cookbook
who most likely has a big fuck
you car and two kids she never looks

at but is always idolizing
(crooked teeth, front of the school choir)
with some accessorized husband most aroused
when fantasizing about finalizing
with online buyers bidding higher and higher,
for all of her low-buttoned blouse,

her fuck me pink push-up bra,
her trimmed asparagus and Laksa
paste and vermin-fucken-celli
noodles and the silken jelly
of her soft, floating, flower-skirted arse.
For me to even dream of her's a farce

but she'll see. For I'm going to have
me a big black Audi with satnav
and leather seats, and I'll burn past her
and every single fucken manager
in this place. I won't be down because of her,
or them. Not even my liaison officer.

He followed me once, got on my bus —
like I wouldn't clock a mumpsimus
with a file chart slitching after me —
so I took him to The Winds where the peelers
won't go, and left him outside Digsy's
front door (and Digsy takes no prisoners)

while I sleeched out the back of the house
to call at Britney's for a bong and tea.
For the next month he couldn't look at me
without his smush turning rufous,
and then he was replaced. Fucken doofus.
I'll show the lot of them. Now, 1, 2, 3 . . .

I'm the safe pair of hands they want me to be,
stacking Pop-Tarts, Branflakes, muesli,
Rice Krispies, Sugar Puffs, Coco Pops,
Crunchy Nut Corn Flakes in the King of Shops.
But when I've shelved the Frosties and Weetabix,
I take my pay, I get my kicks . . .

In a Glass Darkly

Look into my eyes. You're vicious
letters on a furious page, feverous
black ribbons and ravens, dark angels
of cloud-scowl in the sky raining down
hatchets, spanners, Stanley knives, claw hammers,
each raindrop a dropped elevator's scream.

You're a smoker's lungs. You're beaten
meat: cleavered, hung. You're gelatinous
fat on a cold kebab. You're porno music,
a syringe beneath the railway bridge,
a weeping condom squished on the girders
glistened like a swimming lizard's skin.

You're a supermarket aisle packed
with pus-leached, glooping fruit
on shelves that ooze like rancid gums.
You're worms in the puke's tomatoey ghee.
You're an arse-licker's tongue. I'm your mirror.
Look into my eyes and love me.

You're the desert. You're the rizarred
skin and river blindness of the dying,
so you are, the rape of the foreign policies
of the west. I'm your diminishing bent
towards remembrance and kindness.
Look into my eyes and love me.

You're gonorrhoea. You're the beating time-
bomb behind the breast. I'm the dissolution
of all you hoped to be, and you hoped to be
the best, so you did. You're eco-scuzz.
You're all but excuses: 'Because . . . Because . . . '
Look into my eyes. Behold me.

I'm your ghost, so I am. You're the niff
of a turnip fart in a train carriage.
I'm who people think you are, but you'll never be
me, so you'll never. Yet when you go dead water
will drown me. Numb silence and lonely.
Reach through the glass and hold me.

Eloquence

Who would not speak, in their quieter fancies,
as a gannet coasts the blue — to rise, halt
without breaking wing, and kamikaze
downward at breakneck speed, break the salt
water surface, plunge with dead-eyed accuracy
the ice-shock deep, then splash to resurface
with a glittered life writhing in the beak?
Who would not lip such a sentence?
So I would wind myself up to a peak,
lift off from the plains, then relax
and stretch out to soar, dip and turn,
but there'd be some dark slick of pitch to tax
such flight, and I'd splutter, coast-bound and waxed
with the tar-and-gicked feathers of a rigid tern.

On Cloughey Beach

Never so ghosted or small as when alone
on the fragile truce of this strand where sky
and sea stretch what you can hold in the shell
of your ear, your film of skin, between your eyes,
standing on wrack and kelp amid the shoosh
of crisped surf on cockled sand and shore stones.

From further out you feel the heave and thrash
of black-green breakers, bull-headed hellbenders,
white-tipped whale waves, as the swollen lour
and weight of the world in water chunders
while crosswinds birl and breach to scour
and scrub clean the hollow and heft of yourself.

The sea might well wake from its dream and lift
itself up to swallow whole our crust of earth
were it not answered by the hold
of the sky's hoar-blue sift and edgeless width,
the burden of weightlessness it folds
within its centreless limit and drift.

Here as a boy you caught a crab in numb
fingers and toddled, fit to burst, to your daddy —
showed it off, then flung it away. Like a virus,
me-strained in strange created bodies,
we are alien to the elements that host us,
cradle us in their blistered horizons.

Head-staggered by the heights, the cold pit
of the depths, this coast reminds that each scene
through which we move, in which we stand,
is a phantasmal screen through which gleams
a truer world that will shift and distend
forever as we attempt to hold it.

Here we are hard grains of sand blown
over unknown waters, over the dunes,
into the blue melt, to dilate and churn,
reform and return, huddled in kitchens,
workplaces, living rooms, in the confusion
and grace of each other, where we belong.

Here in the swill and erosion, with your face
stung by salt winds under the scurf and loam
of sky, where the yellow-brined bubble-splotch
and green slurp of seaweed dregs your bones,
where your voice is spoomed by water-splurge
and wave-song, you might earn your place.

Everyone a Stranger

What things secrets are when they belong
to someone else! Here I stand, between two
men I do not know. We're in a long
queue in a bank and may never spend two

minutes more with each other again.
The man on my right looks shifty and odd.
He lifts his finger to his nose and nods
to himself time and time again.

It's hard to know what he's thinking.
But when I sneak a peak at the man on my left
I think he might wear a rose-pink G-string
beneath his pinstriped trousers' navy weft.

His eyebrows perch like two black crows.
He has an airplane for a nose.
He has big balloon cheeks, ticker tape lips,
party streamers for fingertips.

He has a spider in his ear. His shoes can fly.
Shoals of fish swim through his eyes.
He sometimes feels like a sink full of dishes.
In the back of his mind three cackling witches

stir bats in a simmering cauldron's ring.
He is a nightingale who cannot sing.
He has a beehive in his heart.
The wheels of his mind stop. And then they start

to drive him slowly round the bend.
Then he's a steam train through the glens
with mountain peaks, crystal skies and wind-chased
snow packed inside his felt-lined briefcase.

His head's a big department store
with thirteen floors and a maze of brands.
At night his maths teacher Mr McClure
chases him through corridors with enormous hands.

He has fire opals and moonstones in his throat.
His wings are silent. In his pocket
he keeps this private note:
The long day hurts, I cannot stop it.

He has coiled springs for knees
but his hopes for the day are already far gone
like sailboats the size of garden peas
adrift on a bobbling horizon.

In a previous life he was a cabbage
root fly perched upon the shoulder of a cow,
and if we grasp the scale and manage
the perspective we might imagine how

this was like being perched on Arthur's Seat,
clutching its pelt of heather and larkspur
as it raised its slow head, its steaming snout,
to look over the rooftops of Edinburgh.

A tiny acrobat extraordinaire
funambulates the tightropes of his string vest.
Veiled beneath his thick canopy of hair
is a vast and teeming rainforest

peopled by orange monkeys. But don't stare.
If you knew what's buttoned-up in his breast
then surely you'd give him a grizzly bear
hug, shake his hand, wish him all the best.

But this shifty man on my right's another matter.
I could tell you nothing about him at all,
as his time comes, he goes forth to the teller,
coughs dryly, and makes his withdrawal.

At Dawn

In the morning I used to moon and mump,
say feck the morning, light up and glugalug
fizzed asprin or Vladivar, rub the balls
of my eyes, google the overnight toll
on the WDM Death Clock and shrug,
slumping back to my sheets and pillowed hump.

But I've given up the moody brooding.
It did no good. Let those down in the dumps
suffer their own radical weather,
wither, interpret themselves forever
and dissolve as the moon's pale sugar-lump
dissolves in the cappuccino-skied morning.

Let me walk in peace past waking streams
of traffic, unbombed streets, sectors and zones,
past terraces that unlock their doors
to release spent dreams of the night before.
These dreams float back onto the street, past phone
masts and cables, swirling up to the tangerine

sun as it unpeels and squeezes out fresh light,
slooshing down to brighten the postman's jig
past the greengrocer who's building pyramids
of melon, his root vegetables splayed like squid
the fishmonger now showers with ice and sprigs
of parsley while swigging from her cool can of Sprite

like the seven billion billion billion atoms
combined in miraculous design beggaring belief
that she is. Let me be bumfuzzled by spires
skewering scalloped clouds like the stairs
leading upwards in *A Matter of Life
and Death*. Let me quake at the momentum

of revved-up Rovers and Renaults, Subarus,
Suzukis and Mercedes, Mazdas, Fiats,
Fords and Hondas as they burn down
four-lane outskirts into the open town's
contraflows, speed-ramps and workplaces that wait
for their workers like cockpits awaiting flight crews

for take-off into teamwork, trade, percentage
points and daily margins, to plot a perfect lunch
with buyers or lovers (this woman has a crush
on the Welsh man from sales, who'll blush
faintly each time that she smiles) of a cut-price munch
box or table d'hôte with musky oak and blackberry-tinted
    vintage.

Let me get loaded on the head-spinning
whiffs and wafts of clashing nations' menus
cooked in the space of one narrow street's
cocktail of kitchens, and feel the browbeat
commis chef's elation as the head chef who's
browbeaten him now pats his shoulder grinning.

Let me look through the fast eyes of a five-
year-old footslogging from her first day at school,
reaching to hold hands with her mother,
each passing person yet another
vivid wonder flashed by in a whirlpool,
all agog as a Mohican snogs a Beehive.

And when the sun volunteers to drop out
of the sky let me lick the head
of a cool deep full pint and be regaled
by yarns doing the rounds: fork-tongued tales
spun to mock or ward off the dead,
the burden to lighten, the rules to flout.

Then feed me with crooning or loud
rondos and reels in a back room
or dark corner of a club. Let the notes
river through, turn my head to a sailboat
careening over chimneys and flumes,
crescendoed up through moon-gaped clouds,

diminuendoed to deeps where we forgive
or forget in an otherworld inches from sleep.
For we return to our own dross and dreck.
For everything ticking either side of the neck,
for each bell that chimes, for everything we keep,
for all that's lost, all that's fine, let me live.

At Dusk

At night I'd pop my cork and rush for the flash
and flush of each instant. My attention
span spun, I'd click-click-click until the click,
not the content, was all. I was a joystick
with no direction but the constant erection
of the appetite. I'd wake with a rash.

But I've pulled the curtains and shut the door
on songs that sing the wow of their moment
to leave nothing but a love-shaped hole
that needs stuffed again, so the world becomes a roll
of advertisements advertising advertisements:
Inside, she reveals all! Next week, she'll show more!

Let me lull in the dim fall of dusk-notes
as crowds fizzle, dissolve and drop
into twilight, for the day's like an old
abandoned plate of food whose cold,
glazed, glutinous remnants are slopped
into the bin of the night's gaping throat.

The rising moon rubs its eye to try to reflect
on the setting sun's peach and violets,
orange flumes and plum-skinned blues that collapse
and vanish in the sky's vermilion relapse
back to nothing but a glister of violent
stars shining like signals of an infinite defect.

Let me flee tick-tock time's paralysis
and float through unplumbed time's pure dead
brilliant book (not like a book when being read,
but like afterwards, when it swims in your head)
of interconnections. The clock looks so sad
because it always knows what time it is;

yet if time ticks on let me not wallow
but face the facts which cluster and collide from
one moment to the next but never join
together as I toss small coins
at a homeless woman, and the next one,
then walk past the rest in a sham of shadows,

silhouettes, shopfronts, lamp posts, car lights
leering like fluorescent chrysanthemums;
past the bobbling torchlights of mobile phones,
warm flat windows, third floor homes,
illuminated cyclists and the white wan
moon-holes on the thigh of a drunk girl's tights.

Let words enter each other the way bold
minds are meant to, and bodies sometimes will,
in the nervous system of a sentence
that tongues and turns, riddled with silence
and the push-pull of sound, so its sense swills
while near-music lingers on the threshold.

By all means let's make love on tables
and chairs, and afterwards, in our return
to binary, feel the melancholy
of having no idea who each other really
is — and under that shadow learn
the true art of consummation, if able.

Let me join the harried who hurry home
to lose or find themselves in children:
wanting to partake of their carnival
of senses we snap and film their marvels
to try to unlock a door, to dwell in
their dawn by proxy, through a picture on a phone.

The better to meet, if only halfway, the wrongs
and rights of the oncoming day, let me
waver between these constant three:
the has-been, the might-be, and the will-be,
when we, the privileged, will wonder who to be,
what to do, as the moon falls to dawn

and we steel to face what we can't forgive,
gather our regrets and forget our shadows.
For each pulse is a rise and fall, a ghost and flame.
For each and every cadence of the falling rain,
for steady ground, for deepened sounds that grow
in the mind, through the air, let me live.

With or Without You

Oh no, she's listening to Yoko Ono.
We were as well-matched as bread
and milk, as Brian Eno and Bono,
but now I'm hanging to her by a thread,
a terminal patient hooked to a drip.
Now my pet names for her are *shit* and *smack*
and I live for a hit: to lick those lip-
glossed lips, be a Moog she might play.
Imagine a millipede on its back,
its thousand legs twitching every which way —
that was my mind when she said her muse was sick
and she was off to discover new music.
Now our love is a derelict studio
where I sit, solo, counting in: *uno, duo* . . .

The Blue-ringed Octopus Found on
South-Australian Shores

It may bring music to the living
room and light,
but the electric cable lies calm across the floor
like slack rope,
like an eel adoze in waters barely living,
if eels ever doze.

Like a tentacle dangled from a dying
conch shell, having turned
the colour of the conch shell at low tide:
an octopus
is hidden like a lung. And he is dying,
who trod there,

toeing the strand's surf and suds and kicking
over speckled pebbles,
over the conch shell that lit to livid yellow
and sudden blue
rings that leapt and bit and left him kicking
his bucket in the sand.

And your skin was pale, but brightly,
like the living
room lit by that cable abuzz with the venom
of its voltage,
and your neck was tethered nightly
by the stark rope

of my self-regard, as I lay back to sing
Take That songs
until your tongue unlipped electric
and I crackled
in your milted eyes' yellow-blue rings
in the dark.

Memory

You wait to see what comes and nothing comes,
no feeling, no unfiled mind-footage
of hot sprawling bright lanes under blue
skies on the outskirts of Los Cabos where scalded
white bungalow walls burst with corallita,
bougainvillea, her neck kissed by neckcurls,
scintillations bangled around the quite
perfect beam of her catch-as-catch-can grins,
glances, thin shoulders and niddle-noddled
head swayed down the turning lane to vanish
where market stalls sell bracelets, fierce chickens,
sim cards, pulses, glittered kills from the sea
while you soak in her aftermath and wait
for something to happen. Nothing happens.

Sifting Through

The plates shifted and her bowls moved,
you hump her dresser into the middle
of the room and waft a white sheet
over it, feeling like a removal

man in the middle of a removal,
then run your fingers over the wallpaper
as if investigating defective
workmanship, or time, as the wallpaper

wafts memories-that wreathe and writhe
down to the shellacked floorboard's dust.
And you're drawn to the wallpaper's rot,
its mingle of oatmeal and cat musk,

as if, if you pressed your finger against
one of those dark blooms of blotch
you might lose it, it might poke through,
then your hand, your wrist, your wristwatch,

your arms to the oxters until you whoop,
whomp and clunter through the bright room
in shorts, clanging straight into the dresser,
back now against the wall, so that its moons

of bowls and plates quiver and jowl —
when she bursts from nowhere, built like a rake,
singing whack fol tha dah will ye dance to
yer parner round tha flure yer trotters shake

with the bright light in her eyes as she scoops
you up and spins and the crisp papered walls
swirl and swell and dizzy-spell
until you pass through all the days or all

the days pass through you, and you come to
with a shiver in the gloam and start to re-veil
the dresser with the sheet, casting a spell like snow
which smothers all that is dream, and all that is real.

The Green Rose

1

Hell won't be full till you're in it,
she said, ye lazy scut, ye big sour-faced
whipster; and in a huff he hoofed it
down the rise, past the stream, thunder-faced
past bogbane, water violet and marsh marigolds,
cress and sorrel spread over the surface
of the stream, effing and blinding as he rolled
with spilling fingers soft Virginian shag —
sucked in deep, blew out slow — and strolled
past blackthorn, barley fields and clay-
crusted hills, where he lay down among white
butterflies, ragweed, dandelions, clags
on a grass bed, green-waved in sunlight,
the wings of crows brooming shadows upon it.

2

Bright light sprawling white cotton clouds
looked like they'd never heard of rain:
some saw in them maps, memory shapes,
continents, faces of demons, gondolas
lazing through sunstreams. He saw sheep
grazing in a greener-than-green field
bedizzled by buttercups carpeted down
to a fizzing hedge, stone path and two
apple trees standing sentry to a view
of the lough, coastline, chopped open sea,
oblivious to things that might have been
or might be, passing lives, the mist and creep
of stolen thoughts, the dead and unborn
drifting, on their backs, counting sheep.

3

Howl' on to your horses for the death of sweet
Jesus, he almost said, almost overpowered,
sensing her sniping behind him, the sweetmeat
stains of her apron caked in buttermilk and flour,
mouth tight shut as a crow's arse, while she looked
down on his backside, his head in the flowers,
where he'd seen a green bloom that he mistook
for a rose for a moment. Once she'd groused and grutched
back indoors he snuck to the barn and took
out the clippers to snick around the edge
of the house, but she stooked her head out
and blared: Don't make a big barney balls of that hedge!,
then went back to griddling hot potato bread
asking where's his mind? what is his head?

4

He dreamed she was a cloud, frayed at the seams,
bits of her floating hither, others thither,
edges wisped, funnelled, whispered and curled,
tentacles feeling for the way the four winds
were blowing. In the evening she would turn
hyacinth, rose, japonica and orange
blossom on a flasket of lemon and blue.
On her best days a big hole would open
in her head and a stairway to marvels
might spotlight through. But mostly she'd be
degged grey, gathering her bits together
in a bloated, grimaced, grave-bellied swell
fit to split open a black harvest of grain,
head-hung children who would forbear her rain.

5

Clegged boots by the door, heavy hair dredged,
battered and bowed by the gravel-hard rain,
sullen and speechless, swilling the dregs
of his tea, she thought him feck-brained,
his head on the table, engrossed with weevils
creeping over fried crumbs and egg-stains
on his thick clacked plate. Why in the name
of the devil's good Da did you go and do a daft
thing like that? she asked, once she'd weaselled
that he'd signed on the straight line of his draft
papers to leave her to the dootering cows —
to leave in his wake a trail of boot-shaped rifts
in the ground: sumped and tumid shrouds
of silt and glit, with his head in the clouds.

6

After he died in July 1916
she received this letter: *Dear Rosie,*
when I get a minute, here and there, I've been
rooted in Leaves of Grass, *which helps me see*
the sweet bay, bluebells and primrose-decked
tumps of our home. I hope you're not lonely.
I dreamt we were lying in a slaking field
edged with yellow-bloomed whin and green
flowers. I think they were roses. You pricked
your pink finger on one and as we leaned
back to watch the clouds you gave it to me
and I kissed it until the gash had been cleaned
among the high rushes of whispering barley.
Regards, with deepest love and sincerity.

7

When next July came she rose to head
out by the whitethorn and poplars, over tinder,
dogwood, docken-strewn paths, while overhead
she could see that white clouds were seething,
furious with ice, shape-shifters, mind-benders,
cheating forms sucking up something from nothing,
sailing over nettles, lungwort and thyme;
and she halted where the stream became a river
by the big elm: among buddleia and woodbine
she took off her blouse, checking nobody
was about, slipped from her skirts, and lowered
herself between two moss-bearded boulders
to flense and flush her still-young body
in the on-gush and go of breaking water.

8

Maybe he dreamed of Lady Dixon Park
or Clandeboye, maybe Killynether,
retreading leaves of grass, stooping to pick
wild tulips, bell heather, thinking 'There will never
be any more heaven or hell than there is now',
watching a felt-pelted bumblebee hover
in circles over a green flower that was new
to him, that was maybe a rose, as he grappled
with the long and the short of it. 'And I know
the amplitude of time' and other unforeseeable
lines swooped and made him think someone stooped
to pluck and blow him through the four winds; that maybe
'I am not contained between my hat and my boots',
no more than the green rose by hip, pricks or loveroot.

On a Cold Evening in Edinburgh

Night falls, as night will,
   out of nowhere and sprawls
black in the thick folds
     and pooled gloom
of itself, and crawls
   into every nook and cranny,
and frost will soon

crackle and slip over the surface
   of things, slick over thoroughfares
and alleyways, paves, cobbles
     and graves, while small moons
of satellites, passenger flights
   and haulage flights patrol
each and every square

inch of the hard-starred
   and static sky like pinhead
toxic blips that scour
     the dark, scar the air.
Fast cats eat the dead
   birds and foxes
rifle through recycling bins

while a bull-necked
   baby bawls and hauls
a breast of milk from bed
     and children dream of guns
and horses against the silhouette
   of hills in the distance.
On a night like this

it's easy to forget little
    we can do or say is likely to avert
fingernails being torn from fingers,
        murder by hunger, genetic malice,
fuel terror that will tear the fatal earth.
    But there can be no turning
our backs on a world that's always turning

to tomorrow's open promise:
    maybe a quick death, maybe slow.
We may never know
        more than the lovesick and pierced teen
who lips blue smoke in an upward
    spiral from her bedroom window
raising wolf whistles from the street below,

but notice how people, like words,
    ache to attach themselves,
unload their burden, tingle and tie,
        fuse and flow into a music
that can only be heard
    in gentle dreams.
Like books on bookshelves we lie

packed into terraces and tower blocks,
    bedsits and bungalows,
listening to passenger trains
        and haulage trains snuffle and cry
in the distance
    bearing untold and heavy cargoes
into the terror and solace of silence

or, for all we know,
    Hull, Bristol, Dover,
to set sail for greater islands
    where the occupied already turn over
to embrace a breeze-kissed
    morning and brace themselves
against the violence

without, the violence within.
    On a night like this
little we can say or do is likely to call
    down the angels,
make the all mighty
    change their minds and suddenly
dedicate their lives to the bliss

of their wives of many long years.
    But to simply cave in
when tomorrow crawls,
    as tomorrow will, out of nowhere,
and slowly lose all trace
    of ourselves; to give up the ghost,
let ourselves fall

and all but drop off the face
    of the earth would be to follow
in the footsteps of the family
    man who flees his family in the face
of the air-strike to save
    his own skin, to break free
and sink or swim

in the edgeless desert and dead time
    of himself; it would be
never to enter the true city;
        never to put our bodies in the line
of ringless fingers, the winds
    of change, their piercing slipstream;
never to crack open our lovesick

and spinning minds
    to feel the solace and bliss
of these streets where we wake to dream,
        dream to wake. On a night like this
it's as if we haven't seen
    them all before: the hurt and the hurtful,
the hunted and unmissed;

legless couples locked together
    singing long dawn songs;
singles who've almost
        given up hoping to throw
their arms around anything but lipless
    visions amid sirens and engines;
the flickering ghosts

of flat screens through windows;
    the widows of the night;
raw girls in tartan minis and tight
        t-shirts under lamp posts;
the breeze and litter's side-street skirl;
    the recently bereaved taking flight,
breaking free in the back of a black taxi

racing past slumpers and stragglers
   ranting, raving, fumbling for a light;
past haulage trains and passenger planes
    breaching the limits of the city
bearing untold and heavy cargoes
   from Taipei, Mumbai, Beijing:
all lovers and loners, watchers

and wardens, captive and free,
   waiting for dark skies to crack
open onto what will be.
    This is what we know.
On a night like this
   the world, the poem, is a ring.
Move like a butterfly, and sting.

Here Comes the Night

Wanting to write a note perfect for you
I was zonked by ten minutes to midnight
and gave up the ghost. So I scribbled blue
nothings on the sheer face of the white,
scrunched it to all but the shape of a ball and threw
it to my darkgreen fuzz of unclean carpet,
putting on a self-circling sad sung song
of lost days instead, cursing my tongue.

Dead beat and burnt out, head shot to hell,
I turned off my dim-watt desk lamp
and lowered myself into the well
of the night, waiting for the black lapped
waters of sleep to ripple and slip and swell
over me. You know those coagulated lumps
you get in a saucepan of granulated gravy
before it's stirred right through? Those lumps were me.

I heard a tin can trickle down empty streets.
I heard televisions flick themselves on in vacant rooms.
I heard a telephone's *dring-dring* repeat, and repeat.
I heard a door hinge creak, then suddenly a slammed boom.
I heard lonely computers receive a tweet.
I heard a CD stick at *Blue . . . Blue . . . Blue*, never reaching
    the moon.
I heard a clock's tick-tock-tick turn *dong . . . dong . . . dong*
and something changed in the air, something wrong.

I awoke and the room was in disfigured shape.
The desk sweated. Walls grew hair. Sour curtains
sipped the night with wrinkled lips. My clothes in a heap
looked a dead man's, while the desk lamp grew talons
and perched like a tawny owl. Repelled by the gape
of blank paper, the pen's insinuations,

I ripped myself off from the bedsheets' sellotape,
donned the dead man's clothes, and made my escape.

Outside stretched a corridor with many doors
vibrating to a bass and drum-thudded sound,
as if giant frogs leapt and belched beneath the floor,
over which keckled the white noise of a thousand
voices — all out of their heads. I could have swore
I lived in a terraced two-up two-down,
but on for a randyvoo, and keen to see you,
I opened the first door and walked straight through.

Half the town was in there, jam-packed and hot.
Johnny Tequila, his trousers much too tight,
tipped his bottle to my lips and didn't stop:
liquor-fire melting my defence against the night.
Huckle-bumped music grabbed at hips and didn't drop.
Glimmer-shimmered mirror balls spangled diamond bright.
It was a helter-skelter hell-raking hullabaloo.
But I moved on, for I couldn't see you.

In the next room I spent time with Johnny Trip
who split me into particles and scintilla,
entered my head, re-jigged its microchip
and left me in a garden of phlox and nicotiana
where electronic stars pulsed their beeps and blips
on nightgrass alive with ghost moths and cicadas
chasing anther-dust, their eyes bright orange moons.
But I couldn't see you, so I tried the next room.

I saw a ladder to heaven without any rungs.
I saw a truck speed through the night on fire.
I saw schoolteachers stalk schools with sawn-off shotguns.
I saw politicians sing 'Imagine' in a naked choir.
I saw the allseeing eyeball of the sun

plucked from its socket in a tangle of wires.
I saw I was wigged-out and caught, in an endless queue,
between losing my place and looking for you.

On the stairs Johnny Debt was trading stocks and shares.
He read my accounts and hollered 'Here comes the rain!'
I asked if he had seen you anywhere?
but he just smiled and offered a payment plan insuring fear
    and pain.
He had a silver watch chain, gold mane of hair,
iPhone, cocaine vial, old school tie. And shit for brains.
But I had to shake him off if I was ever to find
you, so I cursed my name upon his dotted line.

Johnny Fundamental was preparing for war.
He polished his boots, primed his weapons
and swore 'I'll kill until I die'. 'What for?'
I cried. But he picked up his machine gun
and quick-time marched out the door
shouting 'Johnny! Go! Go! Go!' Then he was gone
to make a blood sacrifice in the pine woods.
Oh Johnny find peace. Oh Johnny be good.

The corridor started to resemble a jail.
My journey through the rooms was like a jaunt to the sea
that doesn't make the coast, for I could feel
you'd said hasta la bye-bye to me.
I was a green onion that each room peeled.
I was a gorilla-gram turned up at the wrong party.
I was waiting for a weather change: a barren plain
filling with carcasses, dying for rain.

In the next room illegal aliens danced in cages.
Johnny Pimp made me swear to keep shtum.
Hand on heart he paid them honest wages.

He told me you'd been in my room
but, gurning over some scrunched-up pages,
had vanished quicker than an Irish summer's bloom —
faster than snow melts, the life of a mayfly,
off you flew, quicker than a young bride's nightie.

In the next room I was detained for a week.
Monday I made up some parables and tales.
Tuesday the room hung upon each word I did speak.
Wednesday I burnt their money like a schlemiel.
Thursday I was hounded, branded, paraded as a freak.
Friday I got hammered. Absolutely nailed.
Saturday I was sarcophagized in a worm-crawling tomb.
Sunday I rose again and left that awful room.

By then my tongue had turned to chalk.
I found the next room feeling roundaboutly sick,
but there I bundled into Johnny Vamp. And when I talk
to such a woman, wearing rose-silk lipstick,
clothes so tight you have to gawk,
I can't help but feel more optimistic.
She gave me wine. I drank the dregs.
She stroked my thighs. I crossed my legs.

I was in bits. She was in leather.
She put on Goldfrapp's 'Ooh La La'.
She smooched my neck. I noted the weather.
She turned my knees to pâté de foie gras.
Her belly was pierced. Mine was goose feathers.
She licked my earhole. I said aahhh . . .
She smelled of nutmeg, sage, mayflowers.
I nipped next door for a quick shower.

When I came back she was in a waterbed
with Johnny Matador, flown in from Madrid.

There were oyster shells, green magnums and shed
johnnies draped from the bedstead like chrysalids.
They asked me in among the handcuffs, credit card,
silver glass mirror and rolled-up twenty quid.
But your vision went off inside me like a bomb.
I cried Johnny! Johnny! Where did it all go wrong?

Johnny Blue said 'If you accept for a moment
that life is precious and delicate as an asphodel
or rose, then see some pregnant teenage addict
in a doorway, you've got to hurt until you feel
like a sponge for every other asshole's predicament,
until you yourself feel like an asshole.
So you draw the appropriate lines. Shut your eyes.
But you know that then you begin to die.'

The next room was a simulation console
for re-experiencing past mistakes.
Johnny Regret couldn't be consoled
and sadly sung a self-circling song for heartache
waiting to happen, which swizzled in my earhole.
Why are lost things the only things we can't break?
They manacled me, an invisible cage,
the unknown words I must have scribbled on that page.

Friends tried to buck me up, stop being dour.
Johnny Poontang said when push came to shove
there was always more fish in the fish 'n' chip shop, while
    Johnny Future
asked why I didn't try to write instead for all us
who're here? But I moaned that not writing for you was a
    failure
of love that loves to love the love that learns to love
in time with the latent rhythms of the world.
Johnny Critic said I should try expression without words.

Johnny Violin played an andante,
lifting me over lint bells and lilac
trees into the iris and dragonfly sky,
over wind-ruffled heaths and rilled heights,
down fir-fuzzed and furze-bloomed sides
of rolled mountains, until those wavelight
wedded silk-notes sloughed on hushed tides
in the sluff-wash of whose silence I died.

Johnny Spliff asked 'You know when a tonal beat
repeats in a slow consistent rhythm
and draws you into the hypnotic secret
contained in each pulse, each drop in the ocean,
each star in space, so that chaos retreats,
or at least realigns into portioned design,
silk shot and mellow, shaped around
the mind and body's hinted fusion in that sound;

and then, when that simple rhythm quickens
and varies, tones broaden to chords,
the volume kicks in, and this calm pattern thickens,
wells up like a fizzy drink shaken to burst
through your inner walls with good vibrations;
and then you flow in time with a wave's crest and crash,
with a panther's roar, with the blush of a flower,
with a jumbo jet's soar, in a Mardi Gras of colour;

and then all the machines turn, like, organic, and hate U-
turns into hope that gushes through you, through-othered
with everyone else breaking free, riding their moment
     jackaroo
to that shuffle beat and crude clang and fuzztone clatter
so the undiscovered cosmos that rotates inside you
blows its wad and flops over

in a reamed steamed banana-creamed body-brain-blitzed
    howzat?
Well, why don't you write some words that work like that?'

In the next fourteen rooms respectively
were a Free Presbyterian Church, a nuclear reactor,
a mass grave for polar bears, an anthrax factory,
a shanty town, a genetic enhancement centre,
a prison, a radical mosque, a laboratory
for animal experimentation, a bootleg abattoir,
an investment bankers' boardroom, a plant
for producing pesticides, and a child soldiers' boot camp.

At last I came to the final room — but I was not
out of trouble: for sitting there was Johnny Double.
He'd re-written the scrunched-up note
you'd read. He said 'Look, I helped you out — scribbled
a few gegs. So what? You were doing okay but got
bogged down in complicity and guilt and boo-hoo sniffles.
If someone's huffed over words let them go and suck
eggs. And relax. If you can't laugh, you're fucked.'

I jumped through the window. Down twelve storeys I fell.
I ran for the road, but happened instead
upon a barbwire fence, on the other side of which welled
a harrowed queue of wraiths, groaning and wolf-eyed,
tattered and gowpen, clamouring to dwell
within — kept out by Johnny Border's thin red
line and armed guard, Alsatians and blowlamps,
neat desk of paperfiles, inkpad and stamp.

I ran the rest of the night to a dew-soft lawn,
and on, into a wood of sycamore and pine
where I gashed through wild bramble as the slow-dawned
sky went gaga, glowing garnet and aquamarine,

while I thrashed through fernbrake and blackthorn
until the wood broke where coast winds whined
and wheezed, the sky glummed, and the green-foamed
sea scunged to call its raindrops home.

Down raindrops plupped off the face of things and died.
From woven-coloured wood-shadows Johnny Debt,
who'd trailed me ever since, sat down by my side,
put his arm around me, and together we watched wet
stragglers from the party trek their tired
way home on curving paths, becoming rainswept
and smaller, glistened blurs upon the leaze.
And now I know you won't come back to me

until the earth spins seven times around the moon;
until the clogged air clears and cools and breathes;
until there are no more busts and booms;
until the cows come home; you won't come back to me
until I learn to hold a tune;
until Icarus beats his wings and rises from the sea;
until the summer's in the meadow;
until the valley's hushed and white with snow;

until pigs fly, and water turns to whiskey
or wine, and there's no more sour grapes;
until human nature is no longer a disease;
until we've free money, free love, and a free church in a free
    lay state.
And when you come, it's soft you'll tread above me,
but not until these falling nights abate
and I wake up, figure out what to do,
wanting to write a note perfect for you.

Approaching Your Two Thousand Three Hundred and Thirty-third Night

1

The dusk drapes its fug and weighs on your mind
in the back seat, wound up by what you can't see
as we wind through this darkened braid of streets.
Headlights will do what they can to help find
our way home, while you shuffle and mutter,
your head with the stars, questions that repeat
but hove unanswered in the creeping sea
of night. I'd say you're right: whatever's the matter
in us might well be the same matter in the sun,
each ear of corn, grain of rice, granule of sand;
in humpback whales fluking to sing the depths
of the ocean; and the ocean, and zebras,
and bluebells, and woodswallows; and perhaps,
little head, tired arms, also the moon.

2

When tomorrow comes remember your why? why? why?
and we'll begin with shorelines where gulls arch
consonants in the great vowel of the sky.
We'll walk the city, and woods, where we'll dwell on
dewdripped spiderwebs in the sun, sprunted larches,
couples with dogs poop-scooping on the green,
tall nettles and deep coombs; so when the dark
comes you'll have bearings with which to explore
witches' covens, hard words, war zones, famines,
dragonheads, and the cruel laughter that bores
into your mind. This is what the night is for,
little head, speedy mind. When tomorrow comes
we'll take in what we can from town and park.
Together we will walk through the common.

3

Now that night lets fall her black hair
and watches over you, wraps you in her shawl,
the day drains from you like water from sand
to leave grains of memory, sifting on the shore
of your mind. Such sands of time may fall
through your fingers, sting your eyes, fly everywhere.
But little head, tired arms, try not to dwell on
dead-eyed meanness, why the world is unfair.
I'd say in our dreamtime we woke on an island,
all of us, where there was plenty for all,
but one had a machine gun and made everyone
else slave to the bone for their thrupenny share
while he sat laughing, eating melons,
coining cruel names, fingering his weapon.

4

Little head, tired arms, speedy mind,
let yourself flow with the thrum of the engine.
Driving through the warpled night we can find
our way home, and then worry about heaven.
If there is a heaven it is chained to the earth
like flight to the air, a mirror to light,
air to the ground, rigor mortis to birth.
And if you could look down from the height
of heaven you would see us as loose grains
of rice, or sand, scattered and small
crisscrossed scars on the face of the earth.
We've been sifted through an impassable wall
we will pass through twice. That is all.
You ask what we are for? I'd say imagine.

If There was Time All Day to Wait

in memory of Jim Kelly

Not a minute has passed. If only it was time
to quit, to leave the desk and screen with all
their clocks. You've double-checked the time
for the fifteenth time
in the last ten minutes. If only the day
would clear the scowl of its sky sometime
soon you might find the time
to take a turn about. If she could come too.
If only Harry Kewell could get back to
the form of his prime, his time
at Leeds, before burdened with the weight
of expectation. It's a heavyweight

punch to the whatnots to be made to wait
to no end. If there was money enough, then time
would be no worry. Take the weight
off your feet. But the day's a dead weight
and in your ear you always hear the call
of the future: 'Delayed. Please wait
in queue.' So shuffle your pens and paperweight,
double-check the weather. And what a day
for the Big Man to finally say: 'Today
we have begun to plant and we await
the harvest.' Was that it? The temperature is fair to
middling but the clouds are too

heavy for high hope. Gerrard will have to
play a stormer, carry the weight
of everyone; and everyone will be up to
high do when they hear. Someone should say to
the Big Man: 'Hallelujah. Amen, and about time
too. But what was wrong in '69 or '72?'

Too bad for everyone who's had to
bear him out, too bad for — what did he call
them? — the honoured and unageing dead, for all
that tomorrow is to-
morrow and this, as he says, is today.
AC Milan looked the business last Wednesday.

You heard him rasp and roil one Sunday
by the City Hall, his head raised to
the heavens haranguing shoppers with Doomsday.
Now he says we know not what a day
may bring forth. Back then, he couldn't wait
for those clouds to burst. A new day.
Well, bring it on. A tumour as broad as the day
is long. A time to break down and a time
to build up; a time to keep and a time
to get blootered and blather at the end of the day,
singing 'You'll Never Walk Alone' all
alone, ripping it out, for once and for all.

If only we had another Rush or Fowler, an all-
out finisher who'd prey the entire match-day
for a match-winning through-ball.
Who'd never waver if a chance should fall.
Happiness, his good book says, will come to
him who rewards his enemies as they all
have served him. Which, you thought, meant bugger all
but trouble until now. Thrown like pennyweights
against the rocks of his rage. The deadweight
of his history. If she could phone with the all-
clear you could make the train in time
to walk through the park: arrange a time

to meet her by the gate, and take your time
to walk through the gardens, as if you'd all

the time in the world. For the day
has surely come when there's nothing to
do but get on with it. You can't wait.

8 May 2007

Whiskey

Listen for the whist of unrippled wells
of water, still ponds, dead quiet lakes
you might walk to through wheatfields
and rolled fields of new-flowered flax
into an otherworld of woodland

where boys have stopped playing
soldiers and laid down broken branches
to finger caterpillars, where you might
first have opened lips to feel a tongue
alive in your mouth moons ago.

Lie still by such a low pond and catch
the thistled breeze and shallow flies,
insects twitching in the verbena
and firethorn, the tufted clouds'
degression, a distant Citroën engine.

Better still, go on a winter's night
when you might catch the chattered tink
of your own teeth, the buffets of a barn
owl's wings, shadows that flusker and flitch
over the silver pool's ice and secrets.

For the days are taken and poured
like whiskey into the well of a glass:
for a while we hold the sunset
in hard-worked hands, then drain the glass.
Look through the window on a winter's

night — some might possess your body
but none the hole vented through
that two-way glass, no more than hold
the snow, the lunatic, the vanishing child,
as you lose your reflection in the frost.

For we are swept up in the city's
cashflows and contusions, violet mouths
and japing eyes, until one night,
land-locked in our poverty, caught and cut
up by the glaze of cold eyes, we feel

a sliver of still water, a midnight pool,
and in that fleet stretch of time
before we empty our rusting spirits
into the well of a glass, deep within us,
broken cubes of moonlight tinkle and chime.

Notes and Acknowledgements

The quoted phrases in the last sonnet of 'The Green Rose' are from Walt Whitman's 'Song of Myself'. The speech by Johnny Blue in 'Here Comes the Night' is a quotation, modified to meet the stanza, from the essay 'Astral Weeks' by Lester Bangs, taken from *Psychotic Reactions and Carburetor Dung* (1987).

Ten of these poems, or earlier versions of them, appeared in the pamphlet *The Green Rose* (Clutag Press, 2010), with many thanks to Andrew and Gail McNeillie.

Acknowledgements are also due to the editors of the following publications in which some of these poems, or earlier versions of them, have appeared: *Best of Irish Poetry 2009; Best of Irish Poetry 2010; DIN; Edinburgh Review; Five Points; Forty; From the Small Back Room: A Festchrift for Ciaran Carson; The Golden Hour Book II; Identity Parade: New British and Irish Poets; The Irish Review; Landmarks; Love Poet, Carpenter: for Michael Longley at 70; Manchester Review; Oxford Magazine; Scottish Review of Books; South Carolina Review; The Stinging Fly; Ulster Tatler; Warwick Review; The Watchful Heart: A New Generation of Irish Poets, Poems and Essays* and *The Yellow Nib*.

Many thanks to Peter Fallon and all at The Gallery Press; to my colleagues and students at The University of Edinburgh; and to my wife, family and friends.